Praise for *Wild Delicate Seconds*

These brief meditations are as beautiful for what they don't say as for what they do. Charles Finn does not pad, overreach, or over-emote. His precision accounts of wildlife encounters summon awe, wonder, and magnificence when those feelings are authentically present, but just as readily summon comedy if the encounter was, as Edward Hoagland once put it, "like meeting a fantastically dressed mute on the road." These are not fleeting glances: they are full-on full-bodied face-to-face invocations of the way animals and birds "speak out by saying precisely nothing," uncannily propelling us into "the exact place where the world begins."

—David James Duncan
Author of *The Brothers K* and *My Story as Told by Water*

When I know the name of a creature, Thoreau said, I find it difficult to see. Charles Finn has escaped that disability, and done magic: to summon the moment of encounter with a wild creature without killing that drama with too much mind. The feral moments in this book are deft, alive with exact detail, full, and short. This is a field guide to a different kind of outside, where the wise, wide-eyed child of the self meets ouzel, turtle, fox, and owl. We need more big short books like this one—after reading Finn, you will wander alert, humbled, wise.

—Kim Stafford
Author of *The Muses Among Us: Eloquent Listening and Other Pleasures of the Writer's Craft*

Wild Delicate Seconds is invaluable. Straightforwardly and precisely articulated, it reinforces our sense that we live next door to mysteries while inhabiting profound complexities, and that we should spend time thanking our lucky stars—and Charles Finn.

—William Kittredge
Author of *Hole in the Sky*

In the space of these twenty-nine encounters, Charles Finn invites his readers into a landscape of "uncountable geometries, great silences," a primordial terrain in which "hunger is the beginning of everything." Here, a crane's flight is "the old machinery of the world lifting into the sky." Here, we experience moments so stunning "there is no restarting the heart."

Finn gives us the quality of intense seeing that transcends into insight, seeing that transforms into *vision*. In the encounter with ravens, he reminds us of what poets tell us: "Everything... shouts one thing, and one thing only, 'Pay attention!'" And Charles Finn does. Indeed, he does. His words pay a rapt and rapturous attention.

—Paulann Petersen
Oregon Poet Laureate

Charles Finn's *Wild Delicate Seconds* is like a series of nature photographs taken not by someone who shoots pictures, but someone who takes the time to study the light and the surroundings and bring out the most unlikely aspects of each of his subjects. Finn writes like a poet and views the world around him like a painter.

—Russell Rowland
Author of *In Open Spaces*

Wild Delicate Seconds examines those jeweled instants offering an invitation, brief portals into a more comprehensive, complete, and compassionate universe, instants too often dismissed with a glance. Charles Finn's micro-essays distill keen observation and deep contemplation, articulating an interaction with the world at once inclusive, generous, and instructive.

—Robert Stubblefield

If there were a god and we were its eyes we might see with the simplicity, clarity, and grace that Charles Finn puts into words in *Wild Delicate Seconds*. His meditations on the birds and beasts who inhabit our world as well as his are pungent as wild strawberries, musky as morels, and a treat to be digested in small, memorable bites.

—Annick Smith
Author of *Homestead* and *In This We Are Native*

Wild Delicate Seconds

Wild Delicate Seconds

29 Wildlife Encounters

Charles Finn

Oregon State University Press
Corvallis

The paper in this book meets the guidelines for permanence and durability of the Committee on Production Guidelines for Book Longevity of the Council on Library Resources and the minimum requirements of the American National Standard for Permanence of Paper for Printed Library Materials Z39.48-1984.

Library of Congress Cataloging-in-Publication Data

Finn, Charles C.
Wild delicate seconds : 29 wildlife encounters / Charles Finn.
  p. cm.
ISBN 978-0-87071-655-3 (pbk. : alk. paper) --
ISBN 978-0-87071-656-0 (e-book)
1. Animals--Poetry. I. Title.
PS3556.I495W55 2012
811ʾ.54--dc23
          2011052245

Oregon State University Press
121 The Valley Library
Corvallis OR 97331-4501
541-737-3166 • fax 541-737-3170
http://osupress.oregonstate.edu

For my mother
Sally Stevens Finn
and in memory of my father
Edward Finn

and for my loving wife
Joyce Tinanani Mphande-Finn

I think I could turn and live with the animals,
  they are so placid and self contained;

I stand and look at them long and long.

They do not sweat and whine about their condition;

They do not lie awake in the dark and weep for their sins;

They do not make me sick discussing their duty to God;

Not one is dissatisfied—not one is demented with the mania
  of owning things;

Not one kneels to another, nor his kind that lived thousands
  of years ago;

Not one is responsible or industrious over the whole earth.

—Walt Whitman

We are here to witness

—Annie Dillard

Contents

Preface

In the particular is contained the universal.

—James Joyce

What follow are twenty-nine nonfiction micro-essays, each
one a description of a chance encounter I had with a member
(or members) of the fraternity of wildlife that call the Pacific
Northwest home. Over the last fifteen years I've been fortunate
enough to live in a variety of rural and semi-rural locations
within this same geographic region. This includes Kaslo and
Argenta, British Columbia; Potomac and Stevensville, Montana; and Tumalo, Sunriver, and most recently Bend, Oregon.
It's no surprise that over the years my journals have filled with
descriptions of black bears and bumble bees, mountain lions
and muskrats, elk, pygmy owls, ravens and flying squirrels. What
follows are those stories. With the exception of the snowy owls,
sandhill cranes, and golden eagles, which I specifically went
to see, all of these encounters were complete surprises: as I
came inside from chopping wood a red-shafted flicker flapped
against my cabin window; as I rested in the shade by a river a
red fox suddenly appeared trotting toward me; lost, driving to
a new job, and coming up over a small rise, I saw a hundred
bison on the slope below me, their unmatched authority halo-
ing them in the morning sun. Because of the unexpectedness
of these meetings they held a special quality for me. Always
there was a timelessness, a residue of the sacred, and a lingering
feeling that I was witnessing something spectacular. And I was.
Because these encounters were often so brief (usually just a

matter of minutes, sometimes seconds) it seemed appropriate that I kept my accounting of them equally concise too. For this reason these essays differ from traditional "nature writing." I have chosen not to include background information, specific locations, the natural history of the animal, or even my history with others of its kind, and in this way only the most important details survive, those few shimmering moments I spent lost to the world, alive in the company of these "other nations," as Henry Beston describes them, the wild, feathered, and furred creatures we share this planet with. Finally, I must note that there is very little adrenaline here. There are no maulings. No narrow escapes. It is not that kind of book. Instead, it is a quiet book made up of quiet moments that any of us might have, moments (I hope) with as much grace and dignity as the animals who make up its pages. Ultimately, it is to them I owe a huge debt of gratitude.

Charles Finn
Bend, Oregon
Winter 2010

Black Bear

Black Bear

Bear. It's a big word. Say it in casual conversation and people halfway across the room will stop and cock an ear, setting their drink down or halting a fork in mid-air. Everyone wants to talk about them and everyone wants to see one. They are the denizens of our forests. They have myopic, grandfatherly eyes, bionic noses, and half-dome cartoon ears. Their can-opener claws resemble hay rakes and when they exhale it's with a fetid, composted air. Born in the dead of winter they are blind as new kittens, no bigger than shoes, pink as a ribbon you might win at a fair, nuzzling their mother until the rich milk river flows.

It is October and a sickle moon flies. A black bear crashes through the forest. She is snapping twigs, breaking branches, a pear-shaped hole in the night. She moves in a straight line, head down, shoulders rolling, her massive behind fat from the neighbor's apples pilfered this fall. It's like watching a stone tumble downhill and I stand on my front porch shivering, inarticulate words like startled grouse exploding from my throat.

When the bear stops, she is thirty paces away, her black coat gilded silver by the moon's austere light. I watch her rise on hind legs. I imagine she gives a blackberry roar.

"I've seen the nap you take in the sun," I find my voice and remind her. "I've seen the lilies you digest with such love."

The cone of her nose is pale in the moon's light and she answers with a wag of her head. Then she flops to the ground like a tree coming down. I watch her turn and plow like a fullback into the night. I go back inside.

I put my frying pan down.

Cougar

Cougar

The cougar in my yard is twenty paces away paused in mid-stride, its right foreleg stuck out in front. I am standing in my cabin, sun shining, when its tawny shape passes outside my window.

At first there is only movement, a feline way of creeping low. The cougar slips along the edge of a woodpile, the curvaceous bend of its body as supple as wind. It slinks left to right, no up and down motion, and only when it steps from the shadows does reality come into view. I am looking at *Felis Concolor*—mountain lion, panther and puma, catamount and cougar, courage and kitten magnified in sun-gilded fur. Its coat is a light tan mixed with gray, white under the chin and a white belly that blends into the new snow. I watch as it crosses into the open, shoulder muscles at work like liquid bricks under its fur.

The cougar stops and stands in profile. Large chamomile eyes swivel and look up into mine. Its tail is drooped in an elongated S, shoulders rounded above the sweep of its back. Powder-puff ears are turned toward me and its face is centered around the pink heart of a nose. I can make out the thin lines of its whiskers, also the indent of lips pulled back in their perpetual smile. The cougar lifts its head and dignity oils its fur. It raises a boxing glove paw as if in greeting and I know my one wish above all others is to spend time with one of these cats, to hold and to pet one, to hear one of them purr.

"That lithe swinging of its rhythmical easy stride/which circles down to the tiniest hub/is like the dance of energy around a point/in which a great will stands stunned and numb."

——Rainer Maria Rilke

The cougar sets its paw down ahead in the snow. It lifts the other.

It is starting to drift, to move again like a fog. The cougar is flowing across my yard, meter-long body undulating like water cascading downhill. It wends its way around another woodpile and stops to look at me again, holding the same fringed paw bent at the wrist, pausing before setting it down in the snow. Now it leaps and balances on the stump of a tree, teetering there, four feet bunching together compressing the snow.

We are given these days, don't you know, to do with as we will. I rush outside with my camera. The cougar fixes me with its wine-yellow eyes, the thick rope of its tail lashing once, twice.

Bumble Bees

Bumble Bees

In a series of ragged white orbs, each a stadium of upturned petals, curved and gently bent into a ball, clover covers the lawn. The flowers rest atop vitreous stems, faces tilted toward the sun, their centers a blush of light pink. I'm sitting on the lawn drinking tea. All around me, like oddly painted footballs, black-and-yellow-striped bumble bees move from flower to flower.

The bees move with a heavy buzz. I watch them lift the egg-shaped domes of their bodies. Each time one lands, the head of the clover dips toward the ground, and the bee rides it down, tipped until inverted inside the grass forest that surrounds it. Facing upside down, clutching the petals, it works its way round the edges, abdomen bouncing as it probes for the nectar. When the process is complete, the bee rises, moves sideways, and begins again.

The sun is a white disk in the west. Summer is all afternoon long. The flowers are polite children and the sky a canvas of Monet blues. I sit watching the bees, their inner-tube bodies overinflated, their legs like kinked eyelashes hanging down. The white-noise of their wings soothe me and, as evening approaches, crickets come out to kick in sharp song, and then the frogs, warming up like a hundred small cellos. I stay until the sun sinks below the tops of the trees, until shadows have walked the length of the lawn, until each bee exits on an invisible highway home. Tomorrow, I announce to any who might care to listen, the clover will be here and so will the bees.

I will not mow the lawn.

Ravens

Ravens

I hear the ravens before I see them, their wide corvid wings cuffing the still winter air. They sweep out from behind a spruce tree, turning like black tatters of night against the diesel blue sky. They fly one behind the other, synchronizing their wing beats, expert paddlers canoeing the flat-water air. I watch as they tilt in a great arc, dropping to circle the small clearing. Then they stall. The two brake as one, backpedal, and settle into the branches of an apple tree.

Apples from last fall dangle above them. The fruit is shrunken, rusted to a dull orange, and in the January thaw looks like just ripening tomatoes. As I watch, the ravens jostle and fold themselves into wedges, twisting their necks to show a sheen of gasoline blue. In the chaos of branches the thick slices of their beaks are scythe blades jutting out from their faces, and the black, almost ebony gloss of their feathers are like shawls pulled around them. I watch as these negative-space birds scan the fields, preen chest feathers, call the squirrels terrible names.

This morning the ravens are a matched pair of thieves removing the natural ornaments of the season. They are putting the apples away for the year, storing them in the hollow chests of fir trees, or caching them in ingenious places where no light-fingered raccoon will find them. One at a time, each raven reaches up, opens its beak, and takes a cold sphere down from the blue.

Clown ravens with red rubber noses pump themselves into the air. Tail feathers are folded into spades and cross above the tops of the trees. The ravens can't call with their prizes stretching their beaks, but minutes later they reappear, banking in from the north, knocking the air with their powerful wings. I've hitched myself up onto a rail fence, hooking my boot heels on the second rung below me. Everything, the poets tell us, shouts one thing, and one thing only, "Pay attention!"

The ravens plane down.

Red Fox

Red Fox

The fox, the fox!

—Mary Oliver

With cloud and cloud shadow, sun and then no sun, wind and then no wind, over soft pebbly sand and then quickly in front of the green background of river, the fox came towards me. It drifted, drooping its tail, a spirited flick of each paw before it set it down in the sand.

It was late afternoon and I was seated by the river, leaning against the shipwrecked form of a cottonwood, its roots fanned out around me like the tangled hair of Medusa. The river passed just a few feet away, sunlight ricocheting off its surface and spangling the undersides of leaves. The fox appeared two hundred feet downstream, trotting along the water's edge. It had its nose down, its copper tail wide and scooped out behind it. Its ears were erect, like pointed napkins of fur, and in the afternoon light the insides were painted a translucent pink. I watched the fox coming toward me, feet placed one in front of the other leaving small dimples in the sand like links in a chain.

I scarcely breathed. The fox was fifty feet away, its coat a reddish-brown mixed with gray, white patches on the ears and tail. It moved with its white belly coasting over the ground, its face like an arrow pulled from a quiver. Its pupils were jet black, India ink, what I imagine the black of a tomb to be like. Yet there was a ring of rich earth brown circling the outside, softening them, adding a hint of bizarre, chevalier charm. Here was an old face, I thought, the quintessential wise face of a fox. I could see the full force of intelligence sloping from the ears, down to its eyes, protruding in the sharp snout and nose.

"For the animal shall not be measured by man," writes Henry Beston in *The Outermost House*. "In a world older and more complete than ours they move finished and complete, gifted with extensions of the senses we have lost or never attained, living by voices we shall never hear. They are not brethren, they are not underlings, they are other nations, caught with ourselves in the net of life and time, fellow prisoners of the splendour and travail of the earth."

The splendor and travail of the earth. I didn't move. I never uttered a word.

Water Ouzel

Water Ouzel

He is a singularly joyous and lovable little fellow.

—John Muir

I come down to the river. A ribbon of dark green unspools through the low countryside. Gray corpses of trees collect along the banks, their root masses thrust into the air. Nothing much happens here: leaves decay, beavers dream, small zephyrs of breeze skid along the water's surface, wrinkling it silver. Where a creek enters, a cobble of stones reside, absorbing sunlight and moonlight in succession. In the evening deer wade in, touch coal noses to black current.

The river curdles, turns over, and sinks. Herons stalk leaving strange hieroglyphics pressed into the mud. Fish rise. I come down to the river where the grasses lean in, crushed by the snow, where a kingfisher hovers and spikes into the water, where a merganser floats by. All day clouds come and go and a light snow falls—uncountable geometries, great silences, disappearing into the dark avenue of the river. I watch a water ouzel. The tiny bird dips and dunks and fluffs and preens. It baptizes itself again and again in the frigid water. It is tiring to watch: knee bend, knee bend, knee bend, tail twitch, dunking, tail twitch, kneebendkneebendkneebend, dunking, tail twitch. The cold waters glide by and the little bird hops in, swimming underwater upstream, its wings whirring like propellers turned on. When it hops out, it performs another round of calisthenics and plunges back in. When it reemerges it opens its beak, sings.

When I was a child I'd go each Sunday to mass, climbing the stone stairs that led to the church and entering through its two massive oak doors. There in the knee-creaking silence I'd bless myself, dipping the tips of my fingers into the shallow bowl of water provided. The water would be tepid, soft to the touch, and I'd cross myself, touching my forehead, my belly, and both sides of my chest. That the water was simple tap water I'm sure, but perhaps it was holy, having been blessed. Still, these days, I simply come down to the river.

Bison

Bison

Coming up over a small rise, daydreaming, I was stunned. I stopped the truck and leaned with both forearms on the steering wheel, a long breath, jagged as a saw, escaping in a misty vulgarity against the windshield. Bent to grazing, close to one hundred bison were scattered across the hill below me. They looked implausible, their massive heads and immense shoulders tapering down to ridiculously small hips, hips as delicate and fragile, or so they seemed, as the hip bones of Christ.

I opened the door and stood in the chill air. A single bull, the closest, lifted the dark mass of its head and swung it to face me. In that initial moment it was like watching a tree stump being torn from the ground, a boulder brought to life. Growing up in the east, bison, to me, were mythical creatures, conscripts of history. They existed in textbooks. Now a herd was drifting toward me, sunlight shining through the low cloud of dust kicked up around their knees and glinting off the wet black of their noses.

The bison approached in a slow plod—it was like the aimless roaming of kings. Their coats were deep chocolate brown, shedding in places, the bare hide exposed a charcoal gray. Despite their colossal size they moved with a simple grace, and it was easy to see exactly how much they belonged to the land. In the quiet morning the only sound was the contrapuntal snort of their breathing. It came in short bursts, as if each animal was a train pulling out from a station.

The bison climbed at their molasses pace, each step tapping out a geologic backbeat for the stones. As each animal came broadside to me it would pause and swing the woolly anvil of its head to face me, then fix me with a brown, uncorrupted stare. From twenty feet away they peered out from behind huge shanks of hair and I saw a blue-collar expression embedded in their blunt faces, a resignation and a working man's blues. Like old prize fighters, I could believe they had seen everything.

It took half an hour for the herd to pass, parting around me as if I was a rock in a stream. After they were gone I remained looking at the empty field. I felt washed clean. Brute strength and power are serious narcotics, so too the ultimately delicate and fine. As a species we are drawn to these extremes, the unique and rare lassoing us with their unsuspecting beauty. In the wake of the bison, I sensed a space opening inside of me—I had been let in on a momentous secret. To this day, I have no idea what that secret might be.

But that does not bother me in the least.

Red-shafted Flicker

Red-shafted Flicker

There is a calmness birds bring to people, a steadiness they impart to even the most frenzied of lives. After a long winter their cheery voices are like a tonic we drink with our ears, and the soft flutter of their wings, the quiet mutterings they speak to each other, are like reminders of a distant, gentler time. For a chickadee to land on one's finger is like having the very thing of nature visit the self. Tiny claws dig into the skin, blood and bone rest on our own, there is the inquisitive cock of its head. Such moments leave one feeling slightly askew, as if a part of us was missing or not quite filled. I have both witnessed and felt such an epiphany in the company of birds, their gentle cooing assuaging a loneliness I wasn't aware that I had.

It was late in the afternoon and I'd come inside from chopping wood. Taking off my boots, I was startled when a large bird rose from the back of a chair. It flew directly in front of me, and I cringed when it smashed into a window. Hardly had it dropped with a thump then it picked itself up, flew in the opposite direction and slammed into another.

It was a red-shafted flicker, a member of the woodpecker family. Large, handsome birds, they are smoke-gray and thundercloud blue, a summer storm with orange tail feathers burning through. They're often seen tapping holes in the cedar fascia of homes, and in the air have a distinctive patch of white on the rump, also a seductive, undulating, roller-coaster-like flight. Quickly crossing the few feet that separated us, I threw a towel over its shoulders and picked the bird up in my hands.

It was an adult male. A comma of rescue orange was splashed on each cheek. There was the crescent-shaped bib of black under the chin, and below it a spectacular black and white polka dot chest.

As I smoothed this chest with my thumb, the flicker opened his beak but did not make a sound. Then he cranked his head side to side, carving figure eights in the air. When his eye lit on mine it stayed. The feathers around it were soft gray, a black pupil resting there like a drop of pure oil. I was looking into a minute disc of Japanese lacquer. A chip of ebony broken off from a moonless night sky.

It was a great boon is all I'm going to tell you: to hold that bird and forget my place among *things*. Many times I've come across wild animals in the woods. I know the heightened sense of awareness such encounters can bring. With the flicker there was a great calmness. It spread through the room. Loren Eiseley said, "One does not meet oneself until one catches the reflection from an eye other than human." I nodded and stood. With the flicker I walked outside into the sunshine. I spent thirty seconds holding that bird. I don't think I can be blamed for holding on a little too long, a little too tightly. They were wild, delicate seconds, like the ones that make up childhood. Then I opened my hands.

Sandhill Cranes

Sandhill Cranes

All afternoon I watched the land. When I came to a small rise on a gravel road between nowhere and nowhere, I slowed to a stop and lowered the windows. I sat there like I might be sitting a horse, or at a drive-in, or watching the end of the world—and saw no need to comment. I looked across the stubbled fields and inside the bright circle of my binoculars I didn't question the right of the cranes to be there. I didn't question their beauty.

A pair of cranes stalked the spilled grain from the previous year. In the brown field they wandered with soda-straw legs bent backwards like elbows, corkscrew necks turning over their shoulders. They looked large, larger than birds are supposed to be, the bright patch of red on their heads the only vibrant color for miles around. As they walked, they lifted one foot at a time, lifted one and set it down, paused, lifted the other. They moved across the field in this manner, as if the ground was not what it promised to be, or walking something not to be trusted. When they came to a cow pat they flipped it over. When they flew up it was the old machinery of the world lifting into the sky.

Everyone knows that each day is a grain of sand in an hourglass that once turned over can never be turned back–that the trick, if there is one, is to not let a single grain go by unnoticed. I watched the cranes leap into the air, facing each other and peddling their wings, a silent pantomime of courtship and longing. Beyond them the horizon stretched away for miles, the air above milk blue, growing to a brilliant azure straight above. When the time came the cranes flew away in tandem, necks stretched out, legs dragging behind, and I waited until they were tiny black dots in the void, beauty marks wandering the nameless face of the sky. As I drove away a copper light filled the cab of the truck and I gripped the steering wheel tightly. Another day had slipped by. I could feel it. A tightness between the shoulder blades.

Snowy Owls

Snowy Owls

The purpose of evolution, believe it or not, is beauty.

—Joseph Brodsky

One by one as the afternoon shadows stretched across the winter fields the parliament of snowy owls flew up to sit on the neighboring fence posts. Along the dirt road circling the field, cars were pulled over and spotting scopes set up, thermoses of coffee balanced on hoods like ornaments. Seventeen owls stood in the field or perched on fence posts. They had the attitude of little men, complete and self-contained. Their patience was monumental, as was their posture. Only on rare occasions did they swivel their hunters' heads or blink their telescoping eyes. Resigned to the vagaries of fate and hopeful about the carelessness of mice, they were waiting out their portion of eternity with exceptional calm.

All day the owls hunted in the foot-deep furrows, the tops of their heads showing like errant golf balls. Despite being called a parliament, each kept its own counsel. They would fly from the stands of trees along the edge of the reservoir at dawn and return there in the early evening, or roost far out on the snow-covered ice where distance provided the security they needed. Only then were the day's achievements discussed and the victories of thought their lonely ruminations had produced put forth for debate.

I sat on the hood of my truck with the wind to my back. By six o'clock nearly twenty owls had flown overhead. One landed in the very top of a leafless cottonwood nearby, the late afternoon sun highlighting its feathers. Another flew in front of the snow-covered mountains to the east, the steep walls of the 10,000-foot range lighted in pink.

Beauty is notorious for being only skin deep. It is widely known to be the sole propriety of the beholder. I've even heard it called the hidden reason behind everything, the end-all and be-all of the universe, the very substance of God. If this is the case then Brodsky is right, we are all vehicles for beauty, as well as beauty itself.

That day on the way home I picked up a hitchhiker, a large Blackfeet man by the name of Tony Cutfinger. He told me that shortly after the owls arrived, a naming ceremony was held for a local Blackfeet boy. The boy turned four years old that day, my passenger said, and now goes by the name Snowy Owl.

Western Toad

Western Toad

Shall I compare thee to a summer's day?

—William Shakespeare

Who loves the ugly things of this world? Who loves the cuttlefish? The tree slug? Who loves the toad? I mean, this toad, crossing the midnight road. It has eyes cowled like headlights, Popeye forearms, and skin that sags. It could be a burp from a tuba. Or an evolutionary bad mood.

Tonight I have stopped my truck on a moonless back road. A western toad lies sprawled in the center, motionless as a speed bump. All around me rain falls like a scarf of silk while in my truck's headlights the toad blinks its ancient eyes, blinks and stares, blinks and stares. Its warted skin droops off its backbone like a balloon empty of air and its thick neck bulges. Getting out and squatting on my heels, I see how the light rain pebbles on its back.

The giraffe was a stroke of genius. The swan the work of a poet. But the toad?

The toad is splotched military black and green. It has a slender white line running down its spine, halving it into two meaty sides. With a forefinger I stroke its back and the toad reaches its left front foot forward, at the same time pulling its right back leg up to its side. Then the right front leg is extended and the back left comes forward. I watch as it alternates these strides–oddly balletic, strangely haunting –pushing at the rough tar with its web feet. It takes ten minutes, but I stay until it has reached the far side, until the crossing is completed. Nights like these, rain misting down, I've seen cars speed down this same stretch of road.

They don't even swerve.

Great Horned Owl

Great Horned Owl

Saturday afternoon and six ravens dive bomb a fir tree. They turn, wheeling against the green and azure. Angry screams fill the forest and I hurry along a deer trail, ducking stray branches. When I come out into the open all six birds are airborne at once, each turn, each twist of a wing a calligraphy of violence.

Three-quarters of the way up the tree a great horned owl stands slouched against the trunk. The night warrior is tipped slightly out of plumb, listing like a ship at sea. It stares with eyes locked straight ahead, glowing like headlights left on. It has its wings folded to its sides, its chest streaked black, white, and brown, the tricolors mingling with the branch that it stands on. The tufts of its ears are flattened like an angry cat's and in the mid-afternoon quiet the outrage of the ravens is startling. They holler, but there's no need for translation.

The owl shrugs its shoulders and looks down at its vise-gripping feet. It rocks side to side, each new movement bringing a hailstorm of abuse. A number of times a raven comes dangerously close, almost dashing the owl with its wings, but the owl simply blinks and stares, blinks and stares, ignoring the cacophony around it. Then, tired, bored, sick of the abuse, the owl sidesteps out to the end of the branch, leans forward and launches into the air.

A monster-sized moth glides out from the tree. Air raid sirens go off in the ravens. Forget power, I say, forget greed. History teaches all any of us ever want is to protect our young.

The ravens are in hot pursuit.

Muskrat

Muskrat

Where the river curves in a gentle oxbow a cottonwood log extends out over the slow-moving current, cantilevered five feet above the reflected images of mountains and clouds. I sit straddling the log, perched in the sky, sunlight pinging off the olive green water onto the bottom of my boots. Each afternoon I come here to watch the river and the trees, the kingfishers fish, to delight in the cheerful calisthenics of the water ouzel and the unswerving patience of the herons: to learn something old, I hope—and new.

This afternoon a new face has appeared. It is sleek and intelligent looking, as perfectly formed as a whirled river stone. It is pointed upstream, chin resting on the water as if it was a pillow.

With a shimmy the muskrat moves out into the current, plowing into the green water, huge chunks of sky pushed out of its way. It tacks upstream, crossing at forty-five degrees, its butter-knife tail waving horizontally behind. Halfway across the muskrat dives, disappearing into the murky depths, but moments later it reappears, surfacing ten feet away, a stick drooped crosswise in its mouth and looking like a sagging mustache. The muskrat paddles with its four paws whirling and passes directly below me, beneath my dangling feet. Its coppery fur is streaked brown and soft gray with a smattering of white. I can see every whisker and pointed barb of wet fur, the tufted ears rounded like a bear's, folded back against its oiled head. It is February 14th, and were I so inclined I could drop a penny on its head.

I could drop a valentine.

Painted Turtles

Painted Turtles

They are the size of dinner plates, poker chips, catcher's mitts stacked up in the sun. You see them on hot summer evenings crossing the road, or bobbing in a pond just under the water's surface, their leathery heads like big toes pushed into the sky. They are toy tanks, frowning Buddhas on the boomed ends of logs, the original mobile homes.

It was the middle of June and a dozen painted turtles sunned themselves at the edge of a pond, straddling the outstretched arm of a log. I'd come down the dirt path behind them, crossed on a firm part of ground, and parted the cattails. The turtles had their legs drawn up out of the water and their tails tucked in behind them. They balanced there like saucers, green as Greek olives, crazy yellow lines running across their faces, down their outstretched necks, and over their arms.

I squatted down and watched the turtles laze and bathe; duckweed and contentment spread out all round them. The sky was a blue carapace, cloudless, and the turtles' shells moss green, etched with tiny dark lines resembling the geometric patterns on soccer balls. With their eyes narrowed to slits, they squinted like old men without reading glasses, and like over-burdened mountain climbers they'd scale each other, hooking toed feet on the rims of their comrades. Every so often one of them would fall, toppling the others, and it was like watching a set of cereal bowls tip over. Shells clunking with a dull thud, they'd splash upside down into the green water. No sooner did the turtles hit the water than they would be righting themselves, twisting as skillfully as a cat in mid-air.

Then they'd plane away, a sudden and surprising ballet, silent as shadows disappearing into the inky depths: grace, I was being reminded.

The sun continued its appointed rounds. Water striders performed their miracle. Crouched by that pond, I could not have told you who first came up with the idea of a turtle, or why—but I might have been able to guess.

Elk

Elk

The great hurrah about wild animals is that they exist at all, and the greater hurrah is the actual moment of seeing them. Because they have nice dignity, and prefer to have nothing to do with me, not even as the simple objects of my vision. They show me by their very wariness what a prize it is to simply to open my eyes and behold.

—Annie Dillard

Sunday morning and thirteen elk stand fifty paces away, each its own private and distinct mountain range. They stand motionless, cropping the field grasses at the edge of the forest, milk chocolate shoulders and rear ends pushed into the air. They are massive, giants in this landscape of field sparrows and light. Their trails cross and re-cross in the forest, each path a six-inch trough of last year's leaves pounded back into soil. Along one of them I find a deer skull. Twenty feet in the air it rocks in the wind, a cottonwood branch passing through the now empty universe that once held its eye.

Because the wind is from the north, the elk have smelled me and stampeded into the open. They circle, turn, and spread themselves out in a line. They stand in profile, blinking almond-shaped eyes and turning their ears. Each has an earth-brown hood pulled over its face and down to its shoulders, their backs dipping in a slight saddle that is soft tan, ragged where they're shedding to show a lighter coat underneath.

The herd watches me closely, their white rumps visible against the distant line of dark pines. They are black-nosed and full-bellied, the faintest stub of a tail drooping behind. Their legs taper in strong spindles down to the knobs at their knees and when they run they pick them straight up, forever programmed into stepping over deep snow.

Now a brave soul takes a step forward, lifts its snout, and gives a quick bugle. It's like the yelp of a dog being stepped on. And instantly the herd wheels as one, thundering off in the direction they'd come from, veering in a pair of short zigzags: north, west, then north again. They bunch together as they canter, rocking like merry-go-round horses, and the ground thuds under the punch of their hooves. They run shoulder to hindquarter with their nearest neighbor, steering like a flock of colossal chickadees over the uneven land.

After the short stampede the herd halts, wanders back, and spreads out in a line. For three-quarters of an hour this pattern is repeated: a small flight, the cautious walk back, then the same individual coming forward and giving a bugling call. Finally, friends and dinner waiting, I rise from my position and stand. Cheatgrass bends at my knees. Whatever my life is with its headlines and deadlines, its beer halls and shopping malls, it is also this–thirteen elk facing me across a field of shared silence. The simple fact of their being. This great hurrah.

Chickadee

Chickadee

I would thus from time to time take the advice of birds.

—Henry David Thoreau

A black-capped chickadee is two tablespoons of pluck and vigor in a tent of white and gray feathers, a matching chinstrap and skullcap of black. It is early morning, ten below, and a chickadee moves about a maple, tripping up and down the outstretched arms of the tree. I watch it through the kitchen window, and even from this distance I can make out its bluish-gray legs, the slight coloring of brown on its sides, and the ebony wedge of its beak. With two quick slashes of this beak it swipes its against the branch that it stands on, stropping it much the way a barber would strop an old-fashioned razor. Like all songbirds this chickadee exhibits a chronic kind of *joie de vivre*, and in these cold, early morning hours it is like a homeopathic dose of hope.

I pour a cup of coffee, watch this bird, and am reminded of a story. Once upon a time there was a Buddhist monk who was about to give a lecture. The windows in the lecture hall were open and a petite bird, nondescript or maybe just never described, stood on one of the open sills. Then just as the monk was about to begin, just as the learned and pious old man opened his mouth, the little bird piped up and with a well-rehearsed speech of its own, trilling a string of song into the air–beautiful it was, and sweet, an ordinary extraordinary soliloquy from a pint-sized member of the great outdoors. And who can compete with that? Homer? Virgil? Gautama himself?

No. And the monk recognizing the truth and beauty of what he had heard, bowed to his students and without saying a word rose to leave. Lecture over. Class dismissed.

I cross the kitchen, open the sliding glass door and step into the cold … *Chicka dee dee dee* goes my little friend in the branches above me. *Chicka dee dee dee.*

Deer

Deer

Deer. I see them every day. Their tall white tails disappearing into the woods, their sleek brown coats matching the dry grass from last fall. Every morning they come to the field behind my cabin, stepping with high steps over the uneven ground and lifting black noses to sniff at the wind. Their tall ears turn at the first sound of a snapped twig and their soft brown eyes with their thick dark lashes seem to reflect from a perfect world. Ask the neighborhood dogs about a deer's perfect life and they'll pant excitedly, then grin. Ask the spotted white fawn who drinks from the river and she'll only blink in the sun.

This morning two white-tailed deer. They are mother and daughter, sister and twin, sunlight coating their brown shoulders. They stand at the edge of the clearing, elegant ladies in black heels and fur. As one scans the open spaces for danger the other bows to sample a damp tassel of weed. Now they punch two more steps into the clearing and stand with legs slightly akimbo. As they breakfast their mouths move side to side, their long faces tapered to coal noses with white rings around cinnamon eyes, their lashes curling up like the wingtips of a raven.

John Muir wrote, "Standing, lying down, walking, feeding, running even for life, it is always invincibly graceful, and adds beauty and animation to every landscape—a charming animal, and a great credit to nature."

I step onto the porch. The deer snap to attention—it's like an electric current turned on. The mother pistons a leg to the ground and together they swivel their tall ears to the front.

Then their hides shiver and the white flags of their tails are raised in alarm. In an instant they are streaks of hazel through the obstacle forest; bounding over deadfalls, zigzagging like bees. The black flicks of their heels punish the air behind them. Like dancers they describe parabolas six feet off the ground.

When the deer stop, I walk to the edge of the clearing and hold out my hands, empty, call out my name: Me, a man who lives alone in the forest. Me, a man in need of such friends.

Flying Squirrels

Flying Squirrels

It was as great an act of faith as I will ever see. It was late summer, late afternoon, the sun already down and I sat on my front steps eating dinner. Looking up, I was just in time to see a family of four flying squirrels parachute across my yard, teetering against a backdrop of Beaujolais air.

The squirrels fell on a steep angle from cedar to fir. They looked timid, shaky, steering with constant corrections as you do an old pickup with play in the wheel.

Tunk ...

Tunk, tunk ...

Tunk.

They started from high up, falling as if to impale themselves on the branches below. No sooner did one land than another took off, spread-eagle, casting itself into the air. It was like watching a game of chance, or chase, each squirrel following the exact line picked out by the leader. At the end of each flight they would drop their back legs and sweep up, slapping belly first into the trunk of the tree.

Tunk.

Did they hold their breath as they sailed? Shout a squirrel version of "Geronimo!" and let go? I don't know, but square as kites they flew–stuntmen, stuntwomen–acrobats in a jungle gym world. When they landed they'd scamper straight up the tree, just a tiny clatter of claws and then some bark raining down. Then from the shadows they'd toss themselves into the air, trusting to those few tablespoons of wind cupped in their arms. I sat on my front porch transfixed, a forkful of pasta suspended halfway to my mouth, the glass of wine at my side untouched. No one ever tells us exactly how hard life is going to be—or how rewarding. The squirrels flew away, disappearing deeper and deeper into the forest.

I was ready to let everything go.

Pygmy Owl

Pygmy Owl

And then we'll sit / in the shadowy spruce / and pick the bones / of careless mice

—John Haines

Imagine the sharp stab of the talons to the back of the head. Think what it must be like, stolen, lifted from the fields at dawn. Imagine the mythologies that must belong to the mice, stories of these silent feather-faced gods who drop out of the sky.

It is mid-March and I steer my truck into a gravel pullout on the side of the road. Cottonwoods scratch the low sky and I watch a pair of mergansers bob, upend, and submarine into the lake. I turn off the truck's engine but keep the windshield wipers going. Directly ahead of me, at exactly eye level, a pygmy owl sits clutching the maroon branch of a red osier.

The tiny owl bobs slightly on the thin branch, balancing there like a teardrop against the dark wall of forest beyond. It is six inches tall, alert, a tent of sleek feathers with hula hoop eyes. As I step from the truck I expect it to fly, but instead the owl observes me with a contemptuous stare, fluffing out its chest feathers and slashing violently with a clawed foot at the side of its face. The owl's body is the color of parched dirt, a delicate white speckling its forehead and back. In the center of its face is the hooked beak, crooked like a finger.

The owl rotates its head ninety degrees to the right, back straight ahead, then a full one hundred and eighty degrees backwards. On the back of its head are the false eyes, oval patches of black ringed with white. A light rain falls and the pint-sized raptor cocks its head down. Then, eyes bright as sunshine, it gives a slight hop, a small bounce into space, and opens its wings.

The owl falls on a steep angle, a collision course with the ground, wings spread like a child's paper cutout wings of an angel. The owl lowers its eight lethal talons and disappears into the weeds and there is a short pause, a violent flurry of wings, then it rises. Dangling below it, like a gray question mark, swings the limp form of a mouse.

Vertical ropes of rain descended to drum on the leaves. A yellow warbler cuts through the air like the flame of a candle. The owl returns to the same tree and lifts the mouse above its head. It waves the tiny carcass around, like a victory banner! Now it pins the mouse to the branch that it stands on, and, without asking forgiveness, without asking for pardon, without showing mercy, it tips back, pauses, and sinks its beak deep into the back of the mouse.

I see the mouse's back carved open. I see an eye plucked out and a tiny foot severed and fall to the ground. I see pink flesh in sharp contrast to the dun brown of fur. In the morning light the owl eats furiously, ravenously, a little madly it seems, and if I had not been born in a society that said black was white, that saw only death where there was life, I, too, would have called it beautiful.

Two Fawns

Two Fawns

Both this morning and yesterday evening, while I was sitting outside eating my meals, in the exact quiet and soft light of those hours, a lone deer and two spotted fawns wandered into my yard. Such innocent faces, even in such times as these.

I'd seen the mother a number of times before, standing tall-eared and august in the meadow, or browsing idly on the willow trees in my yard. What I didn't know was that she was parent to two fragile creatures, timorous and knobby-kneed, not even half as tall as the green summer bracken. Looking at me, the two fawns blinked their eyes, batting their lashes as if I were the strangest sight they had ever yet seen.

I was no more than twenty feet away and seated on the grass. Their mother seemed little concerned with this and wandered away over the bank. I was left with her two offspring, two tiny replicas of herself that pranced and played like two frisky colts, spinning in circles and leaping straight up in the air.

For many minutes I was entertained in this way, the fawns darting back and forth, halting abruptly, then dashing in circles again. With each pause they stared straight at me, sometimes stamping their small hooves, I know not, if in frustration that I, too, did not play. Then from some unknown signal or scent they took off in one direction, shooting back in another, lifting themselves effortlessly into the air. I was left with a vision of their white tails raised on the wind and the idea that never had I had two more enjoyable guests to my table, but that in reality, I knew, it was I who was at theirs.

Red-tailed Hawk

Red-tailed Hawk

It is a gray December day and snow blows sideways. A red-tailed hawk perches high in the branches of a ponderosa, the hard-eyed raptor huddled close to the trunk, scanning the snow-covered fields. I approach across open ground, and the hawk eyes me warily, black pupils centered in the yellow egg yolks of its eyes. White streaks run over its forehead and its breast feathers are fluffed out with the cold. As if posing for a coin it turns its head side to side, sharing with me first one, and then the other, of its godly profiles.

I lower my binoculars and remain where I am. The hawk feigns disinterest, drawing a single taloned foot up and tucking it into its chest. This is a lean time of year. Calories are hard to come by. The sharp hook of the hawk's beak glows like a pale incandescence in the colorless landscape and if this bird dreams it dreams of mouse and mouse blood, sunning snakes, and the warmth of a summer thermal cupped under its wings. For reasons of its own the hawk allows my presence, motionless but for its swiveling head. Ultimately, however, it is enough, and the hawk launches itself into air, flying away on a level line, cutting the trees in half. As the hawk crosses in front of me it cranes its head over its shoulder and an unexpected thrill fills me, warming me like a heated stone at the foot of a bed.

Mercy, god only knows, is not at all what we think. Hunger is the beginning of everything. Just ahead of me a tiny set of tracks disappear in the snow, to either side the brush marks of wings.

Three-toed Woodpecker

Three-toed Woodpecker

Three inches off the ground, clipped to the side of a fir tree, chiseling out a hole the size of a dime, a male three-toed woodpecker jackhammers a Morse code through the forest. It is February, ten below, the little bird a wedge of yin-yang black folded on white. He is the size of a diminutive robin, his face striped, fierce, intense like a badger's, white markings zebraing behind oil-drop eyes. A scarf of white feathers is tossed over his shoulders and on his forehead is a bright yellow oval the color of egg yolk. With a woodworker's intensity, the tiny woodpecker raps and then studies, raps and then studies, spiraling counterclockwise up and then down the base of the tree. When he throws his face at the tree it's a fierce swing, like a hatchet coming down.

Compared to his body, his tail is long, V-ed as sharply as a swallow's and braced like a third foot against the trunk of the tree. In the stilled forest his rappings are like tiny gunshots. Now he whips his face over his shoulder and blinks in a fluttering succession, pulling his eyelids front to back. His eyes are dished, reflective, perfect black circles like olives screwed into his head.

All afternoon I follow this little bird from tree to tree, kneeling in the squeaking snow, blowing on my cold hands, my note book lying open on my knees. As I watch he alternates his strikes side to side, angling them in at forty-five degrees until another piece of bark is ejected. He gobbles larvae as he goes, white grains snatched up like sushi rice. In the end he leaps and whizzes away, zigzagging through the avenue of trees, wings whirring like tiny electric motors turned on.

In his absence I'm left with a little sunshine, a little silence, a little snow drifting down—and the question: when, if not now, if not ever, will my life be deemed a success?

Western
Tiger Swallowtail

Western Tiger Swallowtail

They are the epitome of bobbing and weaving. They fly as if in the throes of a drunken fit. They are living pieces of tissue paper, flying pieces of stained glass, gaudily colored crepe-paper creatures that flit and flutter from flower to flower. Even without a wind they dart and dive and dip and rise, careening across the open fields, combining to rise in tiny cyclones, then settling like mini tapestries on the shamefaced and envious heads of the flowers.

It is the first week of July and a fragile light lies easily on the green grass, broken here and there by the puzzle-piece shades of the trees. In the distance a wavering of yellow moves across the field, a tiny flying vibration skipping above the uncut hay like a stone skipping on water. When it reaches the yard it hops the fence, traverses the length of the top rail, and ascends into the waiting arms of a ponderosa. No sooner has it done this than it descends, skimming the shaved grass in a series of sputtering, stuttering, hiccuping glides.

It is a male western tiger swallowtail. Nature's idea of a Rorschach. Like a crazed Baryshnikov it continues its epileptic ballet, dancing right and then left, left and then right, up and then down. Along the way I see a series of fine *jetés*, a number of *entrechats* and a single, glorious *cabriole*. Like a horse that can't find its gait, it circles me twice, then stumbles to the picnic table, a sophisticate with a broken heel. I twist in my seat to watch, undecided if I am witnessing poetry or just motion. When it sets down on a plastic lawn chair I let out a held breath, lean forward, and gape.

Six kinked legs borrowed from a spider and a furry fuse-lage suspended between Paint-By-Number wings–somebody, somewhere, was in a good mood. With a pair of space alien antennae it inches along the back of the chair, sampling the fake grain of the wood. Humility, evidently, is not this but-terfly's strong point. Self-congratulation is in the air. As I watch it folds its wings together, spreads them, and snaps them shut again, six times in all, a half-dozen silent kudos, applauding itself for reasons unknown, but not unimaginable. Its wings are a clearly defined chaos of black and yellow, the four tiger stripes adorning each one like ink stains bled into cloth, and a fringe of black traces the edges, following their fiord-like contours with admirable precision. Beauty is by no means a sin, but it has its price. Just above the eponymous tail, a beak-sized wedge is missing, evidence that the universe is neither subtle, nor blind.

With a will far greater than mine the butterfly once again hoists itself into the air. A sense of urgency surrounds it. "What we choose to fight with is so tiny!" says Rilke. "What fights with us is so great!" On the rough-and-tumble arm of the wind the butterfly staggers, rights itself, and is blown off course again. "Soldier on," I say. "God's speed." The butterfly forges ahead, battling the invisible, and it all ... looks ... so ... familiar.

Osprey

Osprey

There are birds you gauge your life by.

—Terry Tempest Williams

It is a good day—a great day. Seventy degrees and a robin's egg sky, the first buds of the cottonwoods appearing and, on the way here, tulips, gaudy as can be, painting the air with their primary colors. Spring has finally arrived and the river flows by at a stately pace, snowmelt warming to the occasion. I sit on the river bank: shirt off, shoes off, face turned to the sun. Swallows jet fighter above me, each one turning quick as a thought, and even the dower herons appear cheerful, a pair of them soaking their heels where the brown water eddies. Best of all, the osprey are back.

The osprey are back, pacing the skies, slanting into their fish-kill dives, collecting sticks for that monstrosity they call a nest. Not far away a pair nest high atop a platform provided, baling twine and bone woven into the mix. With wings bent at the elbow they leave on hunting and scavenging forays, traveling thirty feet above the water, periodically glancing down as if they have dropped something. Their savagely hooked beaks and bandit stripe of black across the eyes give them a menacing look, one that is not improved by their icy glare. Their white breast feathers act like camouflage, *just a wisp of cloud passing by*. When they spot carelessness, a fish too close to the surface, they stop in mid-glide, and backpedal—the largest humming bird ever seen.

Everything is as it should be. The fish, unseen, rises. The osprey, hunting, slants into its dive. Falling faster than any stone it boomerangs its wings, its black face mask perfect for a killer's. It doesn't matter how many times I've seen this, I am here to tell you there is no restarting the heart, not in this moment. The osprey slams into the water, talons open, wings spread—the afternoon, look around! It's just another flagstone toward forever. When the osprey rises it turns the fish forward, torpedo-wise, and flies off in the direction of the setting sun—victory clenched in its talons. The fish struggles in the burning air, tail fin waving like a broken rudder, and the osprey gives a shivering, shimmering, ghostly air-dance, water shed in all directions.

Bird-fish-sky-water. Life-death-hunger-desire. You can have your movies. You can have your TV.

Mountain Goats

Mountain Goats

I have no doubt that I stand here at the very center of creation. Every fir tree, each of its needles, the movement of wind, all that I perceive and even more that I don't, all resonate with a vital hum. It is the hum of the universe, what the Chinese call the ten thousand things, all of them speaking out, saying precisely nothing. Each is its own center, the exact place where the world begins. The center is where you are standing and the other center is where I am standing.

—Joseph Campbell

It is easy to lose heart in the valleys. There is solace and strength you can gain from high places. It is the last week of September and I've climbed away from the rivers, away from the sheltering shades of the trees and open heat of the fields. I am 9,000 feet above sea level, 500 above treeline. I am in the center of nowhere–the beginning of everywhere. The air is clear, like taking the light of diamonds into my lungs, and a new dusting of snow covers the tops of the mountains in a veil of eye-squinting white. Across the rocky bowl from me a half dozen mountain goats nap, browse, and stare into the midday sun, shoebox faces nosed into the wind. Ignoring or not equipped with vertigo, they crowd out onto the narrow shelves, staring out of black button eyes onto their beautiful and indifferent world.

The goats move from ledge to ledge, sure footed and with enviable ease. Their strong, disproportionately large shoulders propel them up the steep slopes, and their snow-white coats, ending abruptly at the knees, give them the appearance of wearing a mountaineer's gaiters. When they bed down, their coats fan out around them, handsome as skirts, the wispy threads of their beards sideways in the breeze, imparting an image of sagely wisdom and old age.

If there are small pleasures in the world, I believe, by all means take time to enjoy them. I watch the goats for well over an hour. Here, so close to the sky, they engender the landscape. They stare into the wind as if looking for so long has erased all their seeing, and there is a stoic disregard for the elevation, a casual attitude around gravity.

But now the last of the day is bleeding into the sky and the mountains look as if they've been kindled from inside. "The way up and the way down are one and the same," said Heraclitus in the fifth century before Christ. The goats watch me with wary calm, their black stiletto-like horns pointed over their shoulders. I lift myself from the rocks where I sit. Long rays of sunlight pierce the bottoms of clouds. One by one the goats move further up the mountain, drifting like cloud and cloud wrack until disappearing over a distant ridge. I'm left to my own devises, stepping from rock to rock, center to center, all the way home.

Trumpeter Swans

Trumpeter Swans

January 1st and two dozen trumpeter swans sit on their own reflections: preening, resting, dunking their faces into the glass-still water. I watch from a well-hidden blind, the swans passing back and forth in slow unison, each one a prince, a princess, royalty riding a chariot of reflected clouds. As always they are dressed in their ballroom whites and a stateliness surrounds them, their dignity a thing to behold. With grim pride they periscope their heads into the sky, their tall necks thick as my wrist and not a degree off plumb. From oil-drop eyes their face masks sweep out, blending into shovel-shaped beaks, and when they lower their heads they cobra their necks, turning them like a coil of white rope to drape over the snowy heaps of their backs.

Give credit where credit is due. There are no angles or rough edges to these birds. They are all curves and smoothness and grace. Their backs are deeply cleaved, a single furrow running down the middle forming two distinct halves, and in the glittering sun small beads of water roll down the tubes of their necks to pebble on their backs, clear as diamonds. A thing of beauty is not to be ignored, and when the swans leave, honking and slapping wingtips on the water, they fly in front of the wall of adjacent mountains like a string of white pearls. Evolution, we're told, is an on-going process. It is but part way through. Watching the swans, it is hard to believe.

Golden Eagle

Golden Eagle

For to witness majesty, to find yourself literally touched by it—isn't that what we've all been waiting for?

—David Sedaris

It seemed an act of unfaithfulness, to trick those birds out of the sky, teasing them down from their rivers of wind. We looked like disgruntled birds of prey ourselves, fingertips balancing binoculars, elbows resting on knees or held out from our sides like partially folded wings. It was a police stakeout: the camouflaged blinds, the cryptic whispers, the biologists talking to each other via walkie-talkies clipped to their collars. Time and time again I wanted to rest my eyes, my arms, but I stayed at the narrow Plexiglas slit in the blind as long as I could, a zealous acolyte, training my eyes on the far away wind, hoping.

When we caught one, we assembled before the captured bird like pilgrims, gathered there as if before a great oracle. The eagle would look around with great disdain, its brown eyes piercing each of us as thoroughly as a talon. This was no bird. That much was obvious. It never once looked defeated. How backwards it all was. We were in *its* presence, a small feathered god, a chip off the most improbable block. The eagle would open its hooked beak and stick out a red tongue and let out an inaudible scream—and we felt them, our transgressions impale, deep in our chests. Before we released each bird each of us would reach out one last time to stroke its feathers: it was impossible not to. Science, of course, was the reason we were there, but I do not think it was the whole reason. Since then I have read that, by touching a holy man, a sinner hopes for transference of the grace that he lacks.

Canada Geese

Canada Geese

It is mid-December and a loose flotilla of nearly a hundred geese gather at a bend in the river, boating back and forth, lazily upending themselves to pluck weeds from the river bottom. All around them dinner-plate-sized pieces of ice raft past, turning in slow pirouettes, and the river steams, its sinuous black form set to a low boil, great welts of darkness swelling up out of it. I kneel in the snow blowing warm air on my finger. All the while the geese keep arriving.

For the last hour groups of six, eight, and ten have been piloting in, each new group announcing their arrival from a half-mile off. One after the other, I watch them descend on a tethered line, necks stretched out, wings cupped in matching sickles. Always a great ballyhoo of calls rises to greet them, and at the last instant the geese back-pedal, skidding to a short halt by plowing a wide wake with their landing gear feet. They don't wait, but launch into the news of the day, the brass band of their voices rising and falling as if with a tide.

The geese mutter and honk, tossing their voices like rough stones into the sky, the strong yin-yang swoop of their face masks disappearing against the steep river bank. It's not the answers, I have been told, but the questions that go deep. Above the geese the soft colors of the afternoon deepen into a tremendous wound and a gibbous moon is birthed, shadows crawling over the snow to dissolve into the river. More geese keep arriving, each new set making a circling pass overhead, arranging and rearranging themselves in a succession of syllables. Oracles on loan from the north, the geese pass above the deep green of the trees and I can't help but think they are spelling something eternal, perhaps even vital, against the open fields of the sky.

Great Blue Heron

Great Blue Heron

The heron is in the world and I am in the world. It is early morning, mist moves across the open fields of the slough. Above me gray clouds form a blowing, shifting ceiling, while at my feet a dirt path curves like a brown snake around the roots of the trees. All is quiet, only the gentle stirrings of the cattails and the dry click of the reeds. I come here on such mornings with no plan, no desire for the day to be other than it will.

This morning I find myself one hundred yards away from a great blue heron. It looks like a hunched stone, an oval of waiting. The heron stands statue-still in shallow water, two feet tall, silent, reticent, and flower-like, hunkered down among the vertical stems of the reeds like an escapee from a Ming Dynasty painting. In a motion so smooth I would like to applaud, it raises its head, unfolding its accordion neck into a slender S. Like Narcissus it leans out over its reflection. Then it lifts a single foot and places it ahead in the water, slipping it beneath the still surface with hardly a ripple.

A ballerina could not walk more delicately. A bomb disposal expert more carefully. In the growing light pewter water reflects pewter sky and I watch how this flower-bird stalks: horror and beauty are at one in the dawn. The heron hunts with unswerving patience, its hula hoop eyes highlighter yellow, circular as hope. Its head is smooth, domed like the cockpit glass of a jet fighter, its long beak white on top, blue on the bottom, tapered like an immense sewing needle: the heron, nature's idea of a spear-throwing machine. As it moves

I see its chest is a mottled gray and white, its thin legs black and fluted as burnt sticks. When it spreads its wings, six feet of blood vessel blue, I imagine a primordial light from the first days of time escaping into the world. When it folds them again it is like watching smoke being drawn back into its body.

Long knowledge and instinctive skill oil the heron's feathers. I sense an aura of sagely wisdom and old age—a priestliness. In the shadows, cattails float their seeds and I look but cannot see the frog breaststroking to its very own end. Then without warning comes the lightning strike, too fast for my eye to follow, and the heron lifts its sharp beak to the sky. It is like watching a man in a bar reach out and throw back a shot of strong whiskey—and in this moment all is revealed. I see how the heron fits the marsh, how the cattails fit their stems, how the clouds above fit the sky, and the mosses and trees in the forests fit their mountains, and the fish in their rivers fit the water and the bellies of bears. I see how the frog, pierced, fits the beak of the heron, and how the heron, swallowing, fits its hunger. I see how I, awake for what seems like the first time in years, fit my skin and the skin of the morning; nothing without meaning, nothing without consequence, everything fitting everything wholly,

simply,

perfectly.

Credits

Nineteen of the twenty-nine essays in this collection have been previously published, appearing in part or in whole, and often in slightly different forms, in the following publications.

"Ravens," "Black Bears," "Bees," and "Water Ouzel" all appeared in *Big Sky Journal*. "Bison" first appeared in *Montana Magazine* and was reprinted in a slightly different form from that in *Writers on the Range*. "Bison" as it appears in this collection appeared in *High Desert Journal*. "Red Fox" appeared in *High Desert Journal*. "Two Fawns" appeared in *The Naturalist*. "Red-Shafted Flicker" and "Cougar" first appeared in *Inland Magazine*. Both were reprinted in *Inside the Garden City*. "Sandhill Cranes" appeared in *High Country News* and was reprinted in *Inside the Garden City*. "Snowy Owls" appeared in *Flathead Living* and *Inside the Garden City*. "Western Toad" appeared as a 20 line poem in *Wild Earth*. "Elk," "Great Horned Owl," "Chickadee," "Flying Squirrel," "Muskrat," and "Painted Turtles" all appeared in *Inside the Garden City*.